THE FACE OF TRAUMA

Forward

Trauma

Trauma presents itself in the form of traumatic events. Trauma and violence are often used connected or interchangeably; for this discussion, we will use them as a connected entity. Traumatic events can impact the behavioral health of individuals, families, and communities. Traumatic events can include physical and sexual abuse, neglect, bullying, community-based violence, disaster, terrorism, and war (SAMHSA, 2016).

Types of traumatic events as noted on the Substance Abuse and Mental Health Services Administration website include the following descriptions:

<u>Sexual Abuse or Assault</u>

Sexual abuse or assault includes unwanted or coercive sexual contact, exposure to age-
inappropriate sexual material or environments, and sexual exploitation. The Department of Justice's (DOJ) Office on Violence Against Women defines

sexual assault as "any type of sexual contact or behavior that occurs without the explicit consent of the recipient.

Physical Abuse or Assault

Physical abuse or assault is defined as the actual or attempted infliction of physical pain (with or without the use of an object or weapon), including the use of severe corporeal punishment.

Federal law defines child abuse as any act, or failure to act, which results in death, serious physical or emotional harm, sexual abuse, or exploitation of a child.

Emotional Abuse or Psychological Maltreatment

Emotional abuse and psychological maltreatment are considered acts of commission (other than physical or sexual abuse) against an individual. These kinds of acts, which include verbal abuse, emotional abuse, and excessive demands or expectations, may cause an individual to experience conduct, cognitive, affective, or other mental disturbances. These acts also include acts of omission against a minor such as emotional neglect or intentional social deprivation, which cause, or could cause, a child to experience conduct, cognitive, affective, or other mental disturbances.

Neglect

Neglect is the most common form of abuse reported to child welfare authorities. However, it does not occur only with children. It can also happen when a primary caregiver fails to give an adult the care they need, even though the caregiver can afford to, or has the help to do so. Neglect also includes the failure to provide an individual with basic needs such as food, clothing, or shelter. It can also mean not providing medical or mental health treatment or prescribed medicines. Neglect also includes exposing someone to dangerous environments, abandoning a person, or expelling them from home.

Serious Accident, Illness, or Medical Procedure

Trauma can occur when a person experiences an unintentional injury or accident, a physical illness, or medical procedures that are extremely painful and/or life threatening.

Victim or Witness to Domestic Violence

According to DOJ's Office on Violence Against Women, domestic violence is defined as: "a pattern of abusive behavior in any relationship that is used by one partner to gain or maintain power and control over another intimate partner. Domestic violence can be physical, sexual, emotional, economic, or psychological actions or threats of actions that influence another person. This includes any behaviors that intimidate, manipulate, humiliate, isolate, frighten, terrorize, coerce, threaten, blame, hurt, injure, or wound someone." Domestic violence includes violence and abuse by current or former intimate partners, parents, children, siblings, and other relatives.

Victim or Witness to Community Violence

Extreme violence in the community, including exposure to gang-related violence, interracial violence, police and citizen altercations, and other forms of destructive individual and group violence is a recognized form of trauma.

Historical Trauma

Historical trauma is a form of trauma that impacts entire communities. It refers to the cumulative emotional and psychological wounding, as a result of group traumatic experiences, that is transmitted across generations within a community. Unresolved grief and anger often accompany this trauma and contribute to physical and behavioral health disorders. This type of trauma is often associated with racial and ethnic population groups in the United States who have suffered major intergenerational losses and assaults on their culture and well-being.

School Violence

School violence is described as violence that occurs in a school setting and includes, but is not limited to, school shootings, bullying, interpersonal violence among classmates, and student suicide. Youth violence is a serious problem that can have lasting harmful effects on victims and their families, friends, and communities.

Bullying

Bullying is unwanted, aggressive behavior among school-aged children that involves a real or perceived power imbalance. The behavior is repeated, or has the potential to be repeated, over time. Both kids who are bullied and who bully others may experience serious, lasting problems.

Trauma can be a consequence of bullying, which can lead to mental health issues, substance use, and suicide, particularly if there is a prior history of depression or delinquency.

Natural or Manmade Disaster

Trauma can result from a major accident or disaster that is an unintentional result of a manmade or natural event. Disasters can occur naturally (such as tornadoes, hurricanes, earthquakes, floods, wildfires, mudslides, or drought) or be human-caused (such as mass shootings, chemical spills, or terrorist attacks).

Forced Displacement

Forced displacement is a traumatic event that occurs when people face political persecution and are forced to relocate to a new home (as an immigrant or through political asylum) or become a refugee.

War, Terrorism, or Political Violence

Exposure to acts of war-, terrorism-, or political-related violence such as bombing, shooting, and looting can cause trauma in an individual.

Military Trauma

Military trauma refers to both the impact of deployment and trauma-related stress on people who are deployed and their families. Significant numbers of returning service men and women experience mental and/or substance use disorders associated with military trauma and/or military sexual trauma.

Victim or Witness to Extreme Personal or Interpersonal Violence

Victim or Witness of extreme personal or interpersonal violence includes extreme violence by or between individuals including exposure to homicide, suicide, and other extreme events.

Traumatic Grief or Separation

Traumatic grief and/or separation may include the death of a parent, primary caretaker, or sibling; abrupt and/or unexpected, accidental, or premature death or homicide of a close friend, family member, or other close relative; abrupt, unexplained and/or indefinite separation from a parent, primary caretaker, or sibling due to uncontrollable circumstances.

System-Induced Trauma and Retraumatization

Many systems that are designed to help individuals and families can actually cause trauma. For example, in child welfare systems, abrupt removal from the home, foster placement, sibling separation, or multiple placements in a short amount of time can retraumatize children. In mental health systems, the use of seclusion and restraint on previously traumatized individuals can revive memories of trauma. Further, invasive medical procedures on a trauma victim can re- induce traumatic reactions (2016).

The Centers for Disease Control and Prevention continues to collect data concerning the various types of traumatic events and their impact (2018). Now that you have a broadened perspective of the varying types of traumatic events that can cause trauma to an individual or group of people, it is time to discuss the long-term effects of trauma.

Studies of the lifelong effects of trauma have yielded a multitude of results for decades. Historical results range from post-traumatic stress disorder, depression, bipolar disorder, schizophrenia, 'survivor syndrome', (e.g. depression, anhedonia, guilt, somatic complaints), financial loss, and physical injury (Bromet, 1996). Trauma in children can lead to the development of posttraumatic stress disorder as well as to a variety of other psychiatric disorders, including depression, generalized anxiety disorder, panic attacks, borderline personality disorder, and substance abuse in adult survivors of trauma. Research has found that early exposure to stress and trauma causes physical effects on neurodevelopment which may lead to changes in the individual's long-term response to stress and vulnerability to psychiatric disorders. Exposure to trauma also affects children's ability to regulate, identify, and express emotions, and may have a negative effect on the individual's core identity and ability to relate to others (Lubit, Rovine, Defrancisci, and Eth, 2003). Scientists have begun to understand the mechanisms through which the adverse experiences of abuse and neglect, impacting neurodevelopment and psychosocial development, alter child development and produce pernicious mental, medical, and social outcomes (Putnam, 2009). Childhood trauma has lasting effects into adulthood which is well noted in *The Face of Trauma: The Lasting Effect of Childhood Trauma in Adult Years.*

Bromet, E. (1996). Impact of Trauma. *Current Opinion in Psychiatry, 9(2),* 153-157. Retrieved from:

https://journals.lww.com/co-psychiatry/Abstract/1996/03000/Impact_of_trauma.13.aspx.

Centers for Disease Control and Prevention. (2018). *Trauma Statistical Data.* Retrieved from:

htts://www.cdc.gov.

Lubit, R.; Rovine, D.; Defrancisci, L.; & Eth, S. (2003). Impact of Trauma on Children. *Journal of Psychiatric Practice, 9(2),* 28-138. Retrieved from: https://journals.lww.com/practicalpsychiatry/Abstract/2003/03000/Impact_of_Trauma_on_Children.4.aspx

Putnam, F. (2009). The Impact of Trauma on Child Development. *Juvenile and Family Court Journal.*

Retrieved from: https://doi.org/10.1111/j.1755-6988.2006.tb00110.x

Substance Abuse and Mental Health Services Administration (SAMHSA). (2016). *Types of Trauma and Violence.* Retrieved from: https://www.samhsa.gov/trauma-violence/types

Chapter 1. Traumatized to death

Ronald's personal story of the illnesses developed out of childhood trauma and the physical scars created out of emotional abuse is one that is well documented in the book *Diamond* (Hummons, 2017). Ronald's birth was a product of a violent rape.

"Violence has been part of my life for as long as I can remember. I was even conceived in violence according to my mother. I was born on July 12, 1973, at the University of Cincinnati Hospital. My mother was 17 years old. My father, Ronald Barron, known as "Paul" raped my mother. She went with my uncle to visit his friend at his apartment in Over the Rhine in Downtown Cincinnati. It was then, my mom told me she saw Paul for the first time. He was leaning against the kitchen doorway, his arms folded and his face serious. He had a long jerry curl and a mouth full of gold teeth. He was light-skinned with a full nose, and she would have thought him handsome but for the look in his eyes. Chills crawled down her back as he spoke

"Power to the People," he said to her, his voice barely audible. She repeated the phrase; it was the early seventies after all and the Civil Rights Movement was well underway. Her brother asked her about school, and she showed him the report she was doing for her history class on The Great Depression.

My uncle laughed. "Jenni's the scholar in the family."

"Why do you care about American history?" Paul asked, his eyes locking on hers. "Our history dates back to Africa where we were kings and queens." Paul was very militant and was a Black Panther in the late 60's.

"Well, I happen to like…"

"Hey, Paul, relax, man," my uncle said. "I got to go out for a minute. Will you two be alright?"

Paul continued to stare at her. "Yeah, we'll be fine." My mother got up to leave with my uncle but he told her "Wait here baby girl, I will be right back." Reluctantly, my mom sat back down on the sofa and anxiously waited for her big brother to return as promised; except he didn't come "right back."

After my uncle left, Paul moved close to her while his eyes slid up and down her body. "You lookin real good, baby." He put his hands on her shoulders and began kissing her. She tried to pull away, but he only kissed her harder. His hands went under her shirt and reached up her back for her bra. "Stop it," she said. "I don't even know you!" "Shut the hell up." He pushed her onto the couch and held her around the neck with one hand as he pulled her clothes off with the other. She fought as hard as she could before letting go. She let her body go slack like a corpse and looked away, refusing to witness the violence happening to her; she went numb. Paul had no consideration of the pain he was causing her, only the satisfaction of having his way with the little girl he once admired. The feeling of control enticed him almost more than the penetration.

After being violated in one of the worst ways a woman could experience Jenni hid the scars of rape, thinking that if she stayed quiet no one would notice, not knowing that scars weren't the only thing Paul left her with. It wasn't enough for him to leave the scent of the man who violently raped her, he also left his seed." (Hummons, 2017)

My father beat my mother when ever he would get the opportunity. I heard stories about my father stalking my mother after my birth. Eventually he left her alone, but not until he left her completely frozen in fear when it came to him. My mother fell into a crippling depression that left her vulnerable to the advances of my step-father. My grandmother was even fooled by this man and I paid dearly for this union. I was both sexually and physically abused at the hands of my step-father for years.

I attempted to escape to the false security of my biological father. Boy was I wrong. With Paul, my biological father that I was never allowed to call dad, I witnessed the type of violence that could only be compared to those in the military in active combat. In addition to the violence, I was living with a drug addict. I was threatened with rape by an older man and found myself being sexually abused by older women. I even witnessed his father shot in front of me, as well having to live in abandoned buildings because of my father's drug addiction. This was my life until I created an alter ego, Diamond, out of the need to protect the soft child that I really was internally.

"Recent studies have shown that a broad range of traumatic events experienced in childhood including physical abuse, sexual abuse, prolonged hospitalization, and family instability such as parental unemployment or substance abuse have been linked to chronic illness in adulthood stemming from poor immune functioning or poor cardiovascular health." (Mock & Arai, 2011) I am a living and breathing example of these studies.

"The findings indicate that the greater risk of chronic health conditions in adulthood found among those who experienced childhood trauma may be the result of a process of cumulative disadvantage. Specifically, those with a history of trauma in childhood had more chronic conditions in adulthood and this was partially explained by both their lower levels of mental health as well as their diminished socioeconomic resources. " (Mock & Arai, 2011)

In other words, the multiple layers of childhood traumas that I suffered are the direct cause of the medical challenges that I deal with today. I actually have permanent documented brain damage from the many blows that I received to my head as a child by the hands of my step-father. In addition to scaring, my brain is functioning on constant state of heightened activity that was necessary for me to survive on the streets and at home with my mother and step-father. This was a survival method that has made it impossible for me to sleep more than two hours at a time - even years after the trauma had ended. Currently a team of neurologists are working to find solutions to give me some relief. I have been diagnosed with PTSD, had gastric trouble, severe migraines and several other stress related illnesses - that are a direct result of the trauma that I faced as a child.

"Recent clinical and population-based studies suggest that adults who were physically abused as children are more likely to experience migraine than those who were not abused. Reports of childhood maltreatment, especially emotional abuse and neglect, are prevalent in outpatients with migraine. There is extensive overlap of maltreatment types and a high rate of re-victimization in adulthood. All types of childhood abuse and neglect are strongly associated with remote and current depression and anxiety, and the relationship strengthens with an increasing number of maltreatment types." (Headache, 2010) Unfortunately this is something that I have not received much relief from even as an adult.

Chapter 2. The Hidden Scars

The hidden scars of childhood trauma hide the infections that are seen as isolation. This isolations is what breeds shame and creates the toxic breeding grounds that at time manifest physically. The hidden scars are those that are found in the mental health of the survivor of the traumatic experience.

In one study "results demonstrate clear relationships between many traumatic events and, especially, accumulated lifetime trauma experience and both psychological distress and psychiatric disorder. That these relationships persist with temporal priority controlled - and net of the effects of parental psychopathology - suggest the causal relevance of major lifetime events and the conclusion that they represent on important dimension of increased mental health risk. From these findings and from evidence for the significance of traumas in disorder recurrence, it is contended that failure to take account of such events has resulted in the systematic underestimation of the role of stress exposure in accounting for variations in emotional distress and disorder." (Turner & Lloyd, 1995)

Mental health for Ronald was the hardest for him to explain to others. He had created a different personality which is characteristic of having a personality disorder. Ronald battled depression and anxiety all everyday of his life. There were suicide attempts and associations with people that were even more mentally unstable than him. Mental instability was the normal for Ronald and he paid a high price for his norm. This price should have been expected as described by the foreword in "Diamond" (Hummons, 2017)

"Consider, African-American adults are 20 percent more likely to report issues of serious psychological distress than their adult white counterparts. African-American adults living below the poverty line are 3 times (300 percent) more likely to report serious issues of psychological distress than persons of all racial backgrounds living above the poverty line. African-American adults are more likely to experience and report intense feelings of melancholy, hopelessness, and depravity in self-worth than their adult white counterparts. And although African-Americans are less likely to suffer death from suicide than their white counterparts in their teenage life experience, African-American teenagers are more likely to attempt suicide than their white teenage counterparts (8.3 percent versus 6.2 percent).[1] The abhorrent fact that their white teenage counterparts are more successful at committing suicide is no consolation. African-Americans of all ages are more likely to be victims of serious violent crime than are non-Hispanic whites, making them more likely than their white counterparts to meet the Diagnostic and Statistical Manual of Mental Disorders (DSM-V) criteria for post-traumatic stress disorder (PTSD). African-Americans are, as well, 2 times (200 percent) more likely than their white

---

[1] U.S. Dept. of Health and Human Services Office of Minority Mental Health (2016). Mental Health and African Americans. Retrieved from http://minorityhealth.hhs.gov/ohm/browse.aspx?lvl=4&lvlid=24

counterparts to be diagnosed with schizophrenia[2].

"

While I was never diagnosed with schizophrenia - my life has been difficult as an adult.

---

[2] American Psychological Association (APA) (2016) African-Americans have limited access to mental and behavioral health care. Retrieved from http://www.apa.org/about/gr/issues/minority/access.aspx

Chapter 3. Rape Conception

I was a product of rape. There have been a few articles that describe the profound effects that rape has on children that are born as a result of the rape.

Robert T. Muller's article, "Children Born of Rape Face a Painful Legacy" states:

> "A friend of mine once told me that she was the product of her mother's rape. Staring at her reflection in the mirror, she wondered aloud, "Which are the rapist's parts?"
>
> Although rape is profoundly traumatic, relatively little has been said about the lives of children born from it.

As psychologist Andrew Solomon writes in his book, Far From the Tree, children conceived of rape are more likely to suffer from severe psychological disorders, the most common of which are Post Traumatic Stress Disorder (PTSD), depression, and anxiety.

They face many challenges both before and after birth. Research shows that maternal stress severely affects embryological development. Many women who are raped opt to take antidepressants to help them cope, which can harm the fetus."

When trying to understand why the way I was conceived was having a such an effect on him well into adulthood - I read almost every article I could get my hands on. Dr. Vivette Glover wrote in *The Effects of Prenatal Stress on Child Behavioural and Cognitive Outcomes Start at the Beginning* some interesting research that made everything very clear to me.

She stated:

"Many independent prospective studies have now shown that if a mother is stressed, anxious or depressed while pregnant, her child is at increased risk for having a range of problems, including emotional problems, ADHD, conduct disorder and impaired cognitive development. Even the child's fingerprint patterns have been found to be changed, an alteration which may well be linked with changes in brain development.

Both altered brain structure and function have been shown to be associated with prenatal stress. Several studies have shown that all this is independent of possible confounding factors, such as birth weight, gestational age, maternal education, smoking, alcohol consumption, and most importantly, postnatal anxiety and depression. Thus, although the mother's postnatal emotional state and the quality of early postnatal care are clearly important for many of these outcomes, the evidence suggests that there are substantial prenatal effects also.

We have shown that, within a normal population, the children of the most anxious mothers during pregnancy (top 15%), had double the risk of emotional or behavioural problems, compared with the children of the less anxious mothers. Our most recent research shows that these effects persisted until the child was at least 13 years old (unpublished). Most children were not affected, and those that were, were affected in different ways. However a doubling of risk is of considerable clinical significance. There is probably a gene environment interaction, in that a child with a specific genetic vulnerability is more likely to affected in a particular way. The postnatal environment and nature of care can either ameliorate or exacerbate the effects of prenatal stress on child outcome.

It is clear that it is not just toxic or extreme prenatal stress that are important, as several studies have shown that problems such as daily hassles, pregnancy specific anxiety or relationship strain can have an adverse effect on the developing fetus. Effects of acute disasters such as 9/11 have also been demonstrated. Different studies have shown different gestational ages of vulnerability. This may vary for different outcomes. Increased vulnerability to schizophrenia has been found to be associated with extreme stress in the first trimester. The risk for other outcomes, such as ADHD, has been found to be associated with stress later in pregnancy.

The mechanisms underlying all this are just starting to be understood; altered function of the placenta, allowing more of the stress hormone cortisol to pass through to the fetus, may well be important."

Chapter 4. Emotional Trauma

The long term physical effect of emotional trauma

I live with real effects from the trauma that I suffered as a child. Part of the problem is that I didn't really start seeking help until I lost my son to suicide by cop. I didn't realize until after his death that he was dealing with the same issues that I had been coping with as an adult. I had fought for years unsuccessfully in the courts to remove him from the abuse from the hands of his mother's boyfriend. I knew the pain and I fought with everything I had to get him out. I thought like me he had survived because he was an adult - but he was not coping as well as anyone thought.

I initially started this journey to understand what my son was dealing with so I could come to grips with his life ending and him taking a life in the process. As I began to process everything I remembered my own suicide attempt. I understood some of the behaviors that my son's friends were describing to me the deeper I dug into his life. The similarities of his behavior and mine at that age were almost identical in some ways. The only difference is that I self medicated with making money and he self medicated with alcohol and drugs. Both were serious addictions. Mine lead me to prison and my son's cost him is life and the life of someone else.

As I continued to do my own research I found that yet again there was a study that explained exactly why the emotional trauma had physical manifestation.

"One of the greatest challenges to the field of traumatic stress has been the observation that many individuals who coped at the time of their traumatic exposure became unwell at a later date.

Delayed/late onset PTSD is defined in the DSM-IV as a disorder meeting the diagnostic criteria for PTSD which is present after a post-trauma adjustment period of at least 6 months during which diagnostic criteria were absent or sub-threshold. From a theoretical point of view, these are likely to be individuals who have managed to contain their individual distress by adaptive means, but subsequent stresses and/or the natural progression of neurobiology have led to the manifestation of the symptoms. A recent review emphasized the confusion which has arisen from different definitions of delayed onset PTSD.

The existence of this delayed form of PTSD emphasizes how a traumatic experience can apparently lie relatively dormant with an individual only to become manifest at some future point. Many unanswered questions remain about when and how this sub-clinical state is triggered into a full-blown syndrome of PTSD. However, increasingly the evidence would suggest that sub-clinical symptoms leave the individual at risk of progressive activation with further environmental stress or trauma exposure.

The repeated recollection of traumatic memories is a central component of the phenomenological response to traumatic events. Freud highlighted the importance of traumatic memories in his first lecture with Breuer, suggesting that these were the "agent still at work" playing a central role in symptom onset and maintenance. Subsequently, modelling in epidemiological samples has highlighted how traumatic memories account for the relationship between exposure to traumatic events and the symptoms of hyperarousal and avoidance.

The triggering of these memories is also a consequence of fear conditioning mechanisms and these serve to sustain and kindle the increased arousal that is central to the symptoms of PTSD. The disorder arises because some individuals are unable to progressively shut off the acute stress response, which is ubiquitous at times of exposure to such events. From a learning theory perspective, this process is seen as a failure of extinction or new learning in the aftermath of the fear conditioning. Rather, there is a progressive augmentation of the amplitude of the response to reminders.

The effects of stress on the hypothalamic pituitary adrenal axis (HPA) and the autonomic nervous system have long been studied and the regulation of these systems has been referred to as "allostatic load". This refers to the wear and tear on the body in response to repeated cycles of stress. This phenomenon has the potential to be manifest in various ways, influenced by the interaction with other personal and environmental risk factors for disease. Hence, the physiological dysregulation that underpins allostasis represents a final common pathway to disease that can be manifest in various ways.

Particularly in the context of postdeployment syndromes, the link to musculoskeletal symptoms has become a focus of increasing interest. Equally, the role of allostatic load has come to be seen as an important risk for coronary arterial disease and its antecedent risk factors. However, the intermediary role of PTSD has not been the focus of particular interest in explaining these relationships until recently. The emerging body of evidence, which coincides with the real prevalence of PTSD in studies such as the National Comorbidity Survey Replication, suggests that physiological dysregulation associated with PTSD may play a central mediating role in a range of conditions." (McFarlane, 2010)

I didn't know that what I was feeling and what my son was feeling was completely normal based on the horrors that we lived as children.

Which is why I have made it my mission to share what I have learned.

Chapter 5. The physical signs

The hidden scars start to breakthrough to the surface

If only I understood some of the behaviors that indicated that I had serious medical and mental health challenges, I may have been able to get help for myself and then been able to help my son. Instead, I ended up in prison doing time. I had committed a crime, but I was also a victim that had never received the help that I needed after years of abuse and neglect. I don't want anyone else to suffer what I have suffered so I am going to give you the signs.

I had to first identify what is considered a traumatic experience. Anxiety and Depression

Association of America identifies traumatic experience as:

Exposure to actual or threatened death, serious injury, or sexual violation:

- directly experiencing the traumatic events
- witnessing, in person, the traumatic events
- learning that the traumatic events occurred to a close family member or close friend; cases of actual or threatened death must have been violent or accidental
- experiencing repeated or extreme exposure to aversive details of the traumatic events (Examples are first responders collecting human remains;

police officers repeatedly exposed to details of child abuse).

In my case I lived the traumatic experiences as well as witnessed them. Finding out that my son was going through the same thing was a huge blow for me.

I kept researching to get more information so I can understand in the simplest terms. Help Guide describes it as:

"Emotional and psychological trauma is the result of extraordinarily stressful events that shatter your sense of security, making you feel helpless in a dangerous world. Traumatic experiences often involve a threat to life or safety, but any situation that leaves you feeling overwhelmed and isolated can be traumatic, even if it doesn't involve physical harm. It's not the objective facts that determine whether an event is traumatic, but your subjective emotional experience of the event. The more frightened and helpless you feel, the more likely you are to be traumatized.

Emotional and psychological trauma can be caused by:

> One-time events, such as an accident, injury, or violent attack, especially if it was unexpected or happened in childhood. Ongoing, relentless stress, such as living in a crime-ridden neighborhood, battling a life-threatening illness or traumatic events that occur repeatedly, such as bullying, domestic violence, or childhood neglect. Commonly overlooked causes, such as surgery (especially in the first 3 years of life), the sudden death of someone close, the breakup of a significant relationship,

or a humiliating or deeply disappointing experience, especially if someone was deliberately cruel.

Coping with the trauma of a natural or manmade disaster can present unique challenges—even if you weren't directly involved in the event. In fact, while it's highly unlikely any of us will ever be the direct victims of a terrorist attack, plane crash, or mass shooting, for example, we're all regularly bombarded by horrific images on social media and news sources of those people who have been. Viewing these images over and over can overwhelm your nervous system and create traumatic stress.

While traumatic events can happen to anyone, you're more likely to be traumatized by an event if you're already under a heavy stress load, have recently suffered a series of losses, or have been traumatized before—especially if the earlier trauma occurred in childhood. Childhood trauma can result from anything that disrupts a child's sense of safety, including:

> An unstable or unsafe environment
> Separation from a parent
> Serious illness
> Intrusive medical procedures
> Sexual, physical, or verbal abuse
> Domestic violence
> Neglect

Experiencing trauma in childhood can have a severe and long-lasting effect. When childhood trauma is not resolved, a sense of fear and helplessness carries over into adulthood, setting the stage for further trauma. However, even if your trauma happened many years ago, there are steps you can take to overcome the pain, learn to trust and connect to others again, and regain your sense of emotional balance.

Emotional:

> Shock, denial, or disbelief
> Confusion, difficulty concentrating
> Anger, irritability, mood swings
> Anxiety and fear
> Guilt, shame, self-blame
> Withdrawing from others
> Feeling sad or hopeless
> Feeling disconnected or numb

Physical:

> Insomnia or nightmares
> Fatigue
> Being startled easily
> Difficulty concentrating
> Racing heartbeat

    Edginess and agitation

    Aches and pains

    Muscle tension

Trauma symptoms typically last from a few days to a few months, gradually fading as you process the unsettling event. But even when you're feeling better, you may be troubled from time to time by painful memories or emotions—especially in response to triggers such as an anniversary of the event or something that reminds you of the trauma.

While emotional trauma is a normal response to a disturbing event, it becomes PTSD when your nervous system gets "stuck" and you remain in psychological shock, unable to make sense of what happened or process your emotions." (Helpguide.org, 2018)

There are several other things that you can deal with after experiencing emotional trauma. Some of the most common symptoms of psychological trauma may include the following:

Cognitive:

- Intrusive thoughts of the event that may occur out of the blue
- Nightmares
- Visual images of the event
- Loss of memory and concentration abilities
- Disorientation
- Confusion
- Mood swings

Behavioral:

- Avoidance of activities or places that trigger memories of the event

- Social isolation and withdrawal
- Lack of interest in previously-enjoyable activities

Physical:

- Easily startled
- Tremendous fatigue and exhaustion
- Tachycardia
- Edginess
- Insomnia
- Chronic muscle patterns
- Sexual dysfunction
- Changes in sleeping and eating patterns
- Vague complaints of aches and pains throughout the body
- Extreme alertness; always on the lookout for warnings of potential danger

Psychological:

- Overwhelming fear

- Obsessive and compulsive behaviors
- Detachment from other people and emotions
- Emotional numbing
- Depression
- Guilt – especially if one lived while others perished
- Shame
- Emotional shock
- Disbelief
- Irritability
- Anger
- Anxiety
- Panic attacks

Chapter 6

I'm not lazy, I have depression.

Give a detail range of what the symptoms of trauma can develop into

For me depression was not something that was easy for me to snap out of. It wasn't like having a cold or the flu - but my body did shut down like it was the worse cold or flu I had ever experienced. Depression affected every part of my life. My sleep patterns or lack in my case. I was always tired. The fatigue was extreme and I couldn't get a handle on it. Part of it was that I wasn't sleeping but the other issue was that I couldn't get to sleep. My insomnia made things worse - but my insomnia was as a result of the trauma I suffered as a child. I was unable to get my mind to slow down enough for me to rest. I had been living like that for years before I found a doctor that could put the pieces together for me.

People swore that I was just being lazy and refusing to get up. The truth was that I couldn't get up. I was tired and couldn't function no matter what I tried… but once I got up, I couldn't shut down. For me depression didn't happen for just me. It affected every relationship and all my businesses. I was successful at business after I came home from prison because my mind never shut down - but I was not good in a relationship because my mind never shut down.

I am blessed because like 1 in 10 people that suffer with depression - I tried to take my life. I failed in my attempt, but my son was not so fortunate. Which is why this is so important for me to make sure that you understand that although we try our hardest - we can not fight depression alone. We need the help of our family, friends and even medical professionals to fight depression and win.

Those that are fighting depression need you to know the signs even when we don't know how to express them. This is why a support system is so important for those of us that battle depression. We need those that can advocate for us when we don't advocate for ourselves.

Symptoms of depression can include:

- Trouble concentrating, remembering details, and making decisions
- Fatigue

- Feelings of guilt, worthlessness, and helplessness
- Pessimism and hopelessness
- Insomnia, early-morning wakefulness, or sleeping too much
- Irritability
- Restlessness
- Loss of interest in things once pleasurable, including sex
- Overeating, or appetite loss
- Aches, pains, headaches, or cramps that won't go away
- Digestive problems that don't get better, even with treatment
- Persistent sad, anxious, or "empty" feelings
- Suicidal thoughts or attempts

It is vital to help someone who is depressed for you to recognize the symptoms. It isn't likely that we will be able to tell someone that we are depressed. We just know that something doesn't feel right. The part that is the most frightening is when the feelings become normal. That is why it is important for you, our support system to tell us that what we are feeling is not normal. Tell us that you know that we are not faking it or being lazy. We are hurting and you understand and want to help.

Chapter 7. You are what you eat

How trauma affects our nutrition desires and how nutrition affects feed the symptoms

There was a study done in Michigan on how childhood trauma can affect the nutrition and diet of the individual. I would summarize it but it would be best if you just read their summary.

"Trauma and Adverse Childhood Experiences (ACES) can have a life-long effect on individual health status. What is an Adverse Childhood Experience? Adverse childhood experiences (ACEs) are childhood events that negatively impact the child's future. ACEs include: Verbal, psychological, physical, or sexual abuse (witness or victim); Living with household members who are substance abusers, mentally ill, suicidal or ever incarcerated; Living in a household with poor economic resources or with parents who got divorced or separated after the child was born; and Child exposed to racial or ethnic discrimination. ACEs have been linked to a range of poor health outcomes in adulthood, including substance abuse, depression, cardiovascular disease, diabetes, cancer, and premature mortality. ACEs reflect current childhood experiences that impact health and have the potential to predict future individual and intergenerational health and social outcomes. The Center for Disease Control and Prevention (CDC) and Kaiser Permanente conducted one of the largest research studies on the impact of ACES on health and well-being. ACES have been linked to negative health behaviors (e.g. physical inactivity) and the onset of chronic conditions (e.g. obesity, diabetes, and heart disease), and early death in adulthood. The more ACES that occur, the more an individual is at risk for negative health outcomes.

Trauma refers to interpersonal violence (e.g. bullying, and domestic violence), social violence (e.g. war, terrorism), natural disasters (e.g. flood and hurricanes), chronic social stressors (e.g. poverty, racism, and cultural dislocation), and childhood traumas (e.g. neglect, sexual and physical abuse). Low income families with children are more likely to experience traumatic stress as a result of violence and concentrated poverty. For some children, daily activities such as walking to school or riding a bike on the street may produce stress. The percentage of children who have experienced two or more adverse childhood experiences in Michigan (29 percent) is higher than the national average (23 percent). In the state of Michigan, 40 percent of individuals who experience two or more adverse childhood experiences are African American.

Trauma Affected Communities and Trauma Informed Communities are interchangeable terms used to describe low income communities in which residents are affected by trauma. Some of these communities are engaging in community and partnership building activities that promote healthy living programs such as nutrition education, exercise groups, and gardening. Research demonstrates the consequences of stress and positive impact of nutrition in learning, sleep, mood, and energy .The healthy living programs seek to reduce chaos and stress and cultivate community resilience over time. One of the primary concepts of the Trauma Informed Approach model created by Substance Abuse and Mental Health Administration (SAMHSA) is recognizing the signs and symptoms of trauma in clients, families, staff, and others. Providing nutrition education, physical activity classes, and gardening opportunities in Trauma Informed communities, particularly in schools located within Trauma Informed Communities may require new awareness and diverse skills. Skills that equip individuals with the tools to recognize, diffuse, and encourage potentially traumatized individuals. For children with mental health challenges, it is very important to create a healthy relationship with food to decrease the stress and anxiety that food issues often produce. The link between obesity and adverse childhood experiences provide the opportunity for expanding the role of nutrition education in low income communities affected by trauma and exemplifies the significance of increasing knowledge related to choosing healthy foods during stressful events."(MSUE)

Chapter 8. The forgotten memories

The memories that are hidden in our subconscious

Adult Survivors of Childhood Trauma and Recovered Memories
International Society for Traumatic Stress Studies

"The popular press has reported many stories about adults who suddenly remember having been abused as children. Some media reports have emphasized the unusual circumstances or content of such *recovered memories* while other reports have declared that the "recovery" of memories of abuse is false for a variety of reasons. Little in the press, however, has dealt with the science relating to memories of childhood trauma.

Is it Possible to Forget Childhood Trauma?

People forget names, dates, faces and even entire events all the time. But is it possible to forget terrible experiences such as being raped? Or beaten? The answer is yes - under certain circumstances. For more than a hundred years, doctors, scientists and other observers have reported the connection between trauma and forgetting. But only in the past 10 years have scientific studies demonstrated a connection between childhood trauma and amnesia.

Most scientists agree that memories from infancy and early childhood - under the age of two or three - are unlikely to be remembered. Research shows that many adults who remember being sexually abused as children experienced a period when they did not remember the abuse. Scientists also have studied child victims at the time of a documented traumatic event, such as sexual abuse, and then measured how often the victims forget these events as they become adults. They discovered that some people do forget the traumatic experiences they had in childhood, even though it was established fact that the traumatic events occurred.

What Makes People Remember a Traumatic Event after Such a Long Delay?

At the time of a traumatic event, the mind makes many associations with the feelings, sights, sounds, smells, taste and touch connected with the trauma. Later, similar sensations may trigger a memory of the event. While some people first remember past traumatic events during therapy, most people begin having traumatic memories out side therapy.

A variety of experiences can trigger the recall. Reading stories about other people's trauma, watching television programs that depict traumatic events similar to the viewer's past experience, experiencing a disturbing event in the present, or sitting down with family and reminiscing about a terrible shared episode - for some people, these kinds of experiences can open the floodgates of frightful and horrible memories.

Are Recovered Memories Always Accurate?
Scientists believe that recovered memories - including recovered memories of childhood trauma - are not always accurate. When people

remember childhood trauma and later say their memory was wrong, there is no way to know which memory was accurate - the one that claims the trauma happened or the one that claims it did not.

How Might False Memories Develop?

A great deal of laboratory research involving normal people in everyday situations demonstrates that memory is not perfect. Evidence shows that memory can be influenced by other people and situations; that people can make up stories to fill in memory gaps, and that people can be persuaded to believe they heard, saw or experienced events that did not really happen. Studies also reveal that people who have inaccurate memories can strongly believe they are true.

What Kind of treatment is Helpful for Problems Associated with Early Trauma?

Trauma - focused treatments do work, though not all the time and not for every person. It is important for doctors, psychotherapists, and other health - care providers to begin a treatment plan by taking a complete medical and psychiatric history, including a history of physical and psychological trauma. Knowledge about details of traumatic experiences and some of their possible effects can help professional caregivers formulate a treatment approach that might reduce symptoms and improve daily functioning.

How does Trauma-focused Therapy Work?

The point of trauma - focused therapy is not to make people remember all the disturbing things that ever happened to them. People do not need to remember every detail in order to heal. Rather, the goal of psychotherapy is to help people gain authority over their trauma - related memories and feelings so that they can get on with their lives. To do this, people often have to talk in detail about their past experiences. Through talking, they are able to acknowledge the trauma - remember it, feel it, think about it, share it, and put it in perspective. At the same time, to prevent the past from continuing to influence the present negatively, it is vital to focus on the present, since the goal of treatment is to help individuals live healthier, more functional lives in the here and now.

What is the Therapist's Role in Uncovering Traumatic Memories?

Just as it is harmful for people to believe that something horrible happened to them when nothing did, it is equally harmful for people to believe that nothing happened when something bad did occur. Ultimately, the individual involved - not the therapist - must reach a conclusion about what happened in the past. Good therapy shouldn't create or reinforce false beliefs, whether the beliefs are of having been abused or of not having been abused. Competent therapists realize their job is not to convince someone about a certain set of beliefs, but to let reality unfold for each person according to the individual's own experience, interpretation, and understanding. Helpful psychotherapy provides a neutral, supportive environment for understanding oneself and one's past.

Are there Things a Therapist Should Not Do?

Every profession has specific standards of conduct for its practitioners. Based on the current state of knowledge, it is safe to say that some practices are risky. First, a therapist should not automatically assume that certain symptoms mean a person has been abused. Since the same symptoms can often point to a variety of causes, symptoms alone can't provide a proper indication of childhood trauma. Encouraging people to imagine they were traumatized when they have no memory of a traumatic event may promote inaccurate memories. Encouraging such memories under the influence of hypnosis or sodium amytal - 'truth serum' - can further increase the risk of inaccuracies. It also is not appropriate for a therapist to instruct patients to pursue a particular course of action, such as suing or confronting the alleged perpetrator or severing all family ties.

What Should I Do if I Think I may Have Been Abused?

People sometimes suspect they may have been abused as a child, but they can't clearly remember events or are told things that contradict their memories. Trained therapists can provide individuals with the opportunity to look objectively at their suspicions, consider alternative explanations for their feelings, and become informed about the way memory works or can become distorted.

Thus the goal of therapy is to address client - generated concerns about possible childhood sexual abuse, to help clarify the issues related to such concerns, to resolve leftover feelings or ways of behaving that may be due to such traumatic experiences or concerns, and to help each client shift his or her focus from the past to the present and beyond.

Why is it Important to Get Help for Problems Related to Traumatic Childhood Events? Traumas and adversities in childhood may leave scars that last into adulthood and put a person at risk for a variety of difficulties. This is true for all kinds of early traumas, including accidents, disasters, and witnessing violence directed at others, but it is especially true for child abuse and neglect, the victims of which have been studied extensively. Not all childhood trauma survivors experience difficulties in adulthood. However, for many people, it may be important to come to terms with past traumatic events. People who have been in treatment can gain relief from anxiety and depression and are able to stop focusing on the disturbing memories and feelings associated with traumatic childhood events.

Chapter 9. Did I do that?

The choices we make after years of toxic brain wiring

"Negative childhood experiences can set our brains to constantly feel danger and fear says psychiatrist and traumatic stress expert Bessel van der Kolk. He's the author of the recently published book, *The Body Keeps the Score: Brain, Mind, and Body in the Healing of Trauma.*

Children's brains are literally shaped by traumatic experiences, which can lead to problems with anger, addiction, and even criminal activity in adulthood, says van der Kolk. *Side Effects* contributing producer Barbara Lewis spoke with him about his book.

Barbara Lewis: Can psychologically traumatic events change the physical structure of the brain?

Dr. Bessel van der Kolk: Yes, they can change the connections and activations in the brain. They shape the brain.

The human brain is a social organ that is shaped by experience, and that is shaped in order to respond to the experience that you're having. So particularly earlier in life, if you're in a constant state of terror; your brain is shaped to be on alert for danger, and to try to make those terrible feelings go away.

The brain gets very confused. And that leads to problems with excessive anger, excessive shutting down, and doing things like taking drugs to make yourself feel better. These things are almost always the result of having a brain that is set to feel in danger and fear.

As you grow up and get a more stable brain, these early traumatic events can still cause changes that make you hyper-alert to danger, and hypo-alert to the pleasures of everyday life."

This is exactly what happened to me. I had a quick trigger response to anything I would see as danger. It was something that didn't make sense to those around me. On the other side I didn't have any enjoyment for the things that I should enjoy. Even sex was viewed as a business transaction for me. I had sex with women as a means to get them to either do something that I needed or wanted - but there was no pleasure in it for me. I thought that is how everyone felt, until I actually started seeking help. Looking back on the relationships I was in - I didn't love until much later in my life. Even that version wasn't healthy. Now that I know how my trauma as a child had a role in my adult life it made it so important to me to share what I found out about myself with others.

"**BL**: Does trauma have a very different effect on children compared to adults?

BK: Yes, because of developmental issues. If you're an adult and life's been good to you, and then something bad happens, that sort of injures a little piece of the whole structure. But toxic stress in childhood from abandonment or chronic violence has pervasive effects on the capacity to pay attention, to learn, to see where other people are coming from, and it really creates havoc with the whole social environment.

And it leads to criminality, and drug addiction, and chronic illness, and people going to prison, and repetition of the trauma on the next generation.

BL: Are there effective solutions to childhood trauma?

BK: It is difficult to deal with but not impossible.

One thing we can do - which is not all that well explored because there hasn't been that much funding for it - is neurofeedback, where you can actually help people to rewire the wiring of their brain structures.

Another method is putting people into safe environments and helping them to create a sense of safety inside themselves. And for that you can go to simple things like holding and rocking.

We just did a study on yoga for people with PTSD. We found that yoga was more effective than any medicine that people have studied up to now. That doesn't mean that yoga cures it, but yoga makes a substantial difference in the right direction."

I found this to be true for me. I have done yoga and different breathing techniques and it actually has been helping my mind. There are a few other things my doctors want to try to rewire my brain, so I am able to sleep and not be so hypersensitive to certain sounds and smells. I trust the process and I trust my doctors. If I knew what I know now, years ago - I would have gotten help and possibly saved years off of my life. However, I know better now and I am doing everything I can to lessen the effects that my childhood trauma has been having on my adult life.

I may be the face of what untreated childhood trauma looks like, but I am also the face of what it looks like to fight back against childhood trauma.

References

"15 Common Signs of Unresolved Trauma." *HealthyPlace*, Healthy Place, www.healthyplace.com/blogs/traumaptsdblog/2016/06/15-common-signs-of-unresolved-trauma.

"4 Ways That Childhood Trauma Impacts Adults." *Psychology Today*, Sussex Publishers, www.psychologytoday.com/us/blog/mindful-anger/201706/4-ways-childhood-trauma-impacts-adults.

Bellis, Michael D. De, and Abigail Zisk A.B. *Advances in Pediatrics.*, U.S. National Library of Medicine, Apr. 2014, www.ncbi.nlm.nih.gov/pmc/articles/PMC3968319/.

Bornstein, David. "Treating the Lifelong Harm of Childhood Trauma." *The New York Times*, The New York Times, 30 Jan. 2018, www.nytimes.com/2018/01/30/opinion/treating-the-lifelong-harm-of-childhood-trauma.html.

Editor. "Childhood Trauma Leads to Brains Wired for Fear." *Side Effects*, www.sideeffectspublicmedia.org/post/childhood-trauma-leads-brains-wired-fear.

Díaz, Junot. "Junot Díaz: The Legacy of Childhood Trauma." *The New Yorker*, The New Yorker, 31 May 2018, www.newyorker.com/magazine/2018/04/16/the-silence-the-legacy-of-childhood-trauma.

"Definition of Childhood Trauma, Which Includes Abuse." *Blue Knot Foundation*, www.blueknot.org.au/Resources/General-Information/What-is-childhood-trauma.

"Got Your ACE Score?" *ACEs Too High*, ACEs Too High, 10 July 2018, acestoohigh.com/got-your-ace-score/.

Hummons, Ronald. "DIAMOND: The Story of Ronald Hummons Life of Childhood Trauma and the Resilience Created out of Survival (9781977046840): Ronald A. Hummons, Ebony Williams, Nicole Y Riggins, Dr. Raymond H Rufen-Blanchette ThD: Books." *Amazon*, Amazon, www.amazon.com/DIAMOND-

Hummons-childhood-resilience-survival/dp/1977046843.

"International Society for Traumatic Stress Studies." *ISTSS - Clinician Administered PTSD Scale (CAPS)*, www.istss.org/public-resources/remembering-childhood-trauma/what-is-childhood-trauma.aspx.

"International Society for Traumatic Stress Studies." *ISTSS - Clinician Administered PTSD Scale (CAPS)*, www.istss.org/public-resources/remembering-childhood-trauma.aspx.

"Loving a Trauma Survivor: Trauma's Impact on Relationships." *Brickel and Associates LLC*, 3 May 2018, brickelandassociates.com/trauma-survivor-relationships/.

Mimi Kirk @msmimikirk Feed Mimi Kirk, and CityLab. "What Childhood Trauma Does To Young Adults." *CityLab*, 6 Dec. 2017, www.citylab.com/equity/2017/12/the-long-shadow-of-childhood-trauma/547388/.

Peterson, Sarah. "Early Childhood Trauma." *The National Child Traumatic Stress Network*, 25 May 2018, www.nctsn.org/what-is-child-trauma/trauma-types/early-childhood-trauma.

Thompson, Joyce A. "Childhood Trauma and the Mind-Body Connection for Adults." *Therapy for Schizophrenia, Therapist For*, GoodTherapy.org Therapy Blog, 17 Dec. 2013, www.goodtherapy.org/blog/psychotherapy-childhood-trauma-mind-body/.

Oseldman. "Trauma Types." *The National Child Traumatic Stress Network*, 25 May 2018, www.nctsn.org/what-is-child-trauma/trauma-types.

Made in the USA
Monee, IL
16 November 2023